TAKE THIS ONE TO BED

Take This One To Bed

ANTONY DUNN

Valley Press

First published in 2016 by Valley Press
Woodend, The Crescent, Scarborough, YO11 2PW
www.valleypressuk.com

First paperback edition, first printing (October 2016)

ISBN 978-1-908853-74-5
Cat. no. VP0090

A CIP record for this book is available from the British Library.

Cover photographs by Sara Teresa
Cover and text design by Jamie McGarry

Printed and bound in Great Britain by
TJ International Ltd, Padstow, Cornwall

Contents

Acknowledgements

The Adroit Journal (USA), *Alhambra Poetry Calendar* 2009 & 2010, *Bradford Digital Poetry Slam*, *The Cadaverine*, *Days begin...* (Wivenbooks 2015), *A Decade of Poets in Residence 2003 – 2012* (Ilkley Literature Festival 2013), *English Chicago Review*, *The Garden* (OWF Press 2014), *KJV: Old Text – New Poetry* (Wivenbooks 2011), *Lung Jazz: Young British Poets for Oxfam* (ed. Todd Swift & Kim Lockwood, Cinnamon Press 2012), *Magma, New Statesman, The North, Out of Ilkley* (Ilkley Literature Festival 2010), *Poetry and Audience, Poetry London, Poetry Review, The Rialto, Soul Feathers* (Macmillan Cancer Support & Indigo Dreams Publishing 2011), *Southword Journal*, www.poetrysociety.org.uk.

'Advent' was commissioned for *The Guardian* in 2010 by Carol Ann Duffy, who also commissioned 'Eighteen' for *Jubilee Lines* (Faber & Faber 2012). 'In Vitro' was commended in the National Poetry Competition 2011. 'Suburban (ii)' was broadcast in 'The Bards of Whitelocks Bar' on BBC Radio 4 and several of these poems were broadcast on BBC Radio Leeds.

Thanks to all at the Arvon foundation, particularly to Claire Berliner, Oliver Meek and all the staff at Totleigh Barton; to Parisa Ebrahimi and Michael Symmons Roberts for their advice; to Jamie McGarry at Valley Press; to Helen Mort for her astute and generous criticism; to Matthew Hollis for shaping these poems and this collection so wisely and kindly; to Vicki and Milo Dunn.

for my family

'I'll tell you about my life tomorrow.
I'm far, far away from it now.'
MILO DUNN

In Vitro

We found a moment's break between champagne
and seating-plan to bolt into the dark
and dusty mop-cupboard we'd clocked before
and though it had no lock you turned your back
then lifted up your dress and suffered me
to thumb your nicest pants aside and pop
the needle through your skin and push it in.

And this is what I'm thinking of up here:
the Best Man, dazzled, running out of speech,
rooting for the groom and bride, the fruiting
of their marriage bed. I can not make you
out among the guests. You've been gone too long,
all undone in a too-bright cubicle.
Gentlemen and Ladies, raise your glasses.

If you are back and standing at the back,
your glass high, I can guess the tenderness
with which you lift the brittle thing and watch
its little bubbles making themselves out
of nothing, climbing the strings of themselves,
bursting infinitesimally and
becoming, nothing after nothing, air.

Take This One To Bed

then let me have this
moment of your time:

propped against pillows
or curled on one side,

call to mind one clear,
true incident which

has me in it. Hold
that close. Close your eyes.

I miss you too, or
I apologise.

When you've had enough
feel free, turn over.

Honey

Maybe this is how to make my peace
with all my wrongs –

to find the place on the mountain road
from Zagreb to Zadar

where my own was the only car
I'd seen for hours

and find the woman with her honey
in mis-matched jars

on a trestle-table on the verge
and pull up there,

step out into sunlight quickening
the dust and tar

and rosemary, and this time buy some
before driving on.

Chair

A man, one day, shouldered his office chair
and strode along the Valley of the Rocks
then turned to climb the slope to the cliff top

where he set down, neatly level, his chair
above the sea and then retraced his steps,
brought himself back next day and brought with him

a bucket of cement to root his chair
with slaps and pats around its wheels and stalk
and then retraced his steps once more to leave

daylight and night-cold to attend his chair
and in the morning climbed the path and took
his seat above the sea, his back to us.

And he was last seen, upright in his chair
at dusk, as he had been for months, then gone
but for the blink of his fag in the dark.

Someone must assume his office, his chair.
And yes, he is the man I've most admired.
Now settle down, would you? I'm working here.

Boys

I guess it was the track to Bardney Woods
before we trekked off into fields of frost,
so tall amid that landscape when we stood,
lost, beside a crow hung from a post.

Perhaps it was the staling-biscuit reek
we blamed the far-off sugar factory for
that made us sure the tops around our feet
were beets, a field of sweets unmade and raw.

I don't suppose I would have been the first
to pull one up and brush it off and bite
the bitter root, spit out a clot of earth,
but I was one. We cursed the shrinking light,

struck out along a way we hadn't come
and startled gangs of crows to beating black
and couldn't slake that taste nor tell, at home,
why only almost all had made it back.

Eighteen

York, 25 – 26 June 1991

These are the longest days. Exams are done
and we are indolent and steeped in sun
and somewhat drunk by dark, one couple gone
to fumble, inexpert, beyond the lawn
and the reach of the bonfire, when someone
cries 'Midnight'. It's the twenty-sixth of June.
I am sung to an end; I am begun.
> *Tifanny, Rachel, Joby, Simon,*
> *Michael, Sally, Charlotte, John.*

We lie back in the ordered grass as smoke
riddles the machinery of trees, tracks
east across the fields, and east. Someone cracks,
'It might be ours to go and not come back,
drafted to Sarajevo or Iraq.'
We can't make each other out. No one speaks
but someone pokes the fire and scatters sparks.
> *Adam, Isla, Sophie, Kinshuk,*
> *Indraneil, Becky, Mark.*

We have exhausted everything that burns
bright and quick and the fire has guttered down
to a smallness of embers before dawn.
A blackbird starts at a rumour of sun.
The day will come along the green dark lane
with processing cars to carry us on.
We will not be this way again.
> *Tifanny, Rachel, Joby, Simon,*
> *Michael, Sally, Charlotte, John.*

Ward

Oh, Sister, what are we to make of this?
There's a man in scrubs and four-day stubble;

all the blue-gowned afternoon he's been there,
in the lobby, in the way, at the doors,

stepping on the mat to spring them open
then standing back to see them sliding shut,

though he isn't watching. He's staring out,
spooking patients shuffling in from their smokes.

It's hard to tell with him silhouetted
in the light that way, but he's *listening*,

look. Speechless. As if his life depended.
Reception say they've called Security.

The noise is driving them to tears – the doors'
glide acquainting them, for all the world,

with a gasp, a sift of emptying breath.
Someone praying, over and over, *Ssshh*.

Animal Rescue

To say nothing of all the moths and wasps
I've been opening windows for;

the sheep headlocked in the wire
of a fence,

the newt in the slippery inch
of a dog-bowl of rain,

the spider coming off and off
its wall of death in the kitchen sink

and the bat flopping the living room floor
in a straight-jacket of dust, cobweb and hair.

·❧ ☙·

I have angled your skulls
impossibly free,

poured you out into colour-matched weeds
at the edge of the pond,

offered you into a wineglass and out
to the forest of herbs,

and taken you into my own
unravelling hands and worked you loose

in this borrowed house; let you go
on the slopes by the buzzard tree.

Now, who's coming for me?

Spider Hours

'Every human being, while asleep, ingests an average of eight spiders per year.' Anon.

If we're going to swallow the line
about spiders, let's have the whole truth.

Once they've abseiled through your trachea
they strike out into the labyrinth

of bowels and bronchi, your arteries
and all the little-known routes through you,

paying out a silken, sure way back,
each a tiny Theseus hunting

trophies – your retroviruses or
carcinogens, scoops of fat or tar,

particulates of your griefs, regrets
or grudges, your bad dreams, your night-sweats –

tucking each dead-headed threat under
one of their arms and then hauling out.

Before we wake they're gone, disposing
safely of those little parts of us,

who-knows-where, extending our life-spans
by years we can not count. Our blessings.

They've been said to bind a broken heart
with silk. You make what you will of that.

While You Were Sleeping

She did not leave her warmth behind in bed,
go down the stairs and on down through the mist
between the valley's morning trees, nor step
into the river where the water calms
about itself, nor keep on walking till
her hips, her breasts, her throat were under, hold
her head beneath the surface longer than
she thought her breath would hold to watch her limbs
becoming weightless. And she did not climb
again the valley and the stairs, nor pour
herself back into bed, nor spill but one
cool kiss onto your skin, nor will she, when
you wake, be able to explain the footprints
pooled around the house, nor where she might have gone.

Leeds to London

In a carriage quite deserted and bright
south or north of Newark, late at night

as house- and street-lights constellate and pass
my temple buffers at the window-glass.

Suffer me to sleep on the luggage shelf.
I can see that I am beside myself.

Suburban

i. Crisis

You'll find it finds you
at the kitchen sink

with the radio
twittering, perhaps –

the RSPB
announcing the news:

coal tits have crept in
to their garden birds'

top ten this April.
After all the mess

that the weather made
with the flooded beds

and the torn-through hedge
just look! Look at them!

So many of them
mobbing the feeder,

bright and beautiful
enough to make you

weep, washing up and
putting things away.

Close

i

There's a field I have to cross
no wider than the span
of the human voice.

It will be evening by then
and every stem of grass
in my wake broken.

Portrait of Poet in Tea Room

He should know better than to face himself
into a mirrored corner, in his state.

He has a poet's eye and by the time
the tea-things are arrived and set out straight

he's gone and memorised the whole damn room –
found himself, no less, at the cooling end

of a minuscule affair of glances
with a harassed mother several tables off.

I know. I've been studying in the glass
how he's so intimately learned his place

that when he stands, turns out to face the world
he'll find it, staggered, all the wrong way round,

upset some tables, spill apologies
to folk he does and doesn't recognise.

Crossing the Line

Let's wake the night porter for a corkscrew,
and stop the lift between two floors

for a sour-tongued slug of gooseberry wine.
We've wavered at the funicular view,

zipped up its slope; its sliding doors
have chaperoned us up its straight-up line.

Let's slide out, now, through the night-rain
in mistletoe- and cherry-light,

dare each other down parallel tracks; trails
we've trammed today. This high-wire walk again,

our netless act; and how we might
stay on, or slip together off the rails.

You, You

Awake at five, and you're not listening
to two owls calling back and forth since four,
although you can't not hear them. And it's not
the early start that's made you so damn sore

but envy of the one who, sending out
his note, repetitive and clear and pure,
is every time so promptly answered back,
who can not know the meaning of *unsure*.

It's not just that the signal's so poor, down
here in the valley, as it was for your
five hours on the train, but that, for all
your calls and texts, your phone's done nothing more

than spell the slow time since she Liked (but made
no comment on) the Facebook snap of you,
at last, two days ago, arriving here.
And one of you will crack, and you know who.

Take Off

Before he woke, his clothes crept from his wardrobe, drawers
and laundry bin, or picked themselves up from the floor,

co-ordinated in familiar groups, glanced at
their loose ensembles at the mirror and went out:

a dozen or more invisible men, each one
transparently him, but single-mindedly gone;

one – linen suit, white linen shirt and wedding shoes –
to Lit. events with listening girls and all-night booze

and one – his flip-flops, swimming shorts and baseball cap –
with empty suitcase to the airport in a cab.

His jeans, his cardigan and raincoat caught the bus
to town and back, day in, day out, without a fuss.

His hiking boots, his combats and his anorak
strode off into the hills without once looking back.

So some did this and some did that while he, at last,
learned to accommodate his dressing gown's distress,

his pants and t-shirt balled against his naked side,
all day, in bed and *sobbing*, he'd have almost said.

Leaving

i. Goldfish Bowl

The way this feels may be the way
the goldfish felt the day that Gabe,
at two, more quickly than we knew
got his hands around a glass deep
and gold with twenty-year Ardbeg
and plopped it neatly in their bowl;
one flipping out in an upturned
tumbler, one ranging crazed in all
that lonely space, and both of them
astonishingly drinking in
the sour draught in their atmosphere.

Leaving

ii. Household Chemicals

One clean stroke of an arm beneath the sink
and bottles of disinfectant and bleach
come dundering out onto the floor; such
a colourful blunder. You didn't think
how heavy they'd be, lugged in plastic bags
along the towpath through Good Friday snow
towards the tip when your gloves are at home,
unpaired, and buried in an unmarked box
stacked in the hallway, perhaps, soaking up
from the carpet a trodden-in slush.
The loops of Polythene are harsh
around your fingers. You could let them drop
in any bin or right here in the street,
but this is your responsibility;   ·
to put your many harms out of harm's way,
to dispose safely of all that could hurt.
Though when you find the tip snow-bound and shut
it's no wonder to see you weep at it,
and almost make the choice to take the lot
out, here, unscrew their caps, up-end and wait
to suck up whatever reaction starts
between Benzisothiazolinone
and Methylisothiazolinone,
Hydroxides and Polycarboxylates.

This is very likely to go badly.
Here on the pavement is where you come to.
Oh, Antony, Antony, I hardly
recognized you. I hardly knew you.

Leaving

iii. Left

Things have been leaking from the house
for weeks now and the water's off
while something underneath the sink
is out of true.
              And you forget
how wide the rooms are that you've filled
with books and albums, furniture
until you pack them up, until
you test the echo of a name
against the walls.
              And Easter Day
is wide and bright outside with snow
and I have one last thing to solve
before I go:
              beneath the globe
of light-shade in the living room
our pair of goldfish in a bowl
who never turned a corner
in their lives, who know no better
than to be about each other,
soundless, open-mouthed.

Leaving

iv. Departures

Two hours in this overcrowded lounge
and for no reason I'm replaying
the moment I tumbled from the cab
and through a waiting room and found you
listing on a gurney, your face masked
with blood and the skin split wide across
the new rift in your skull.

And how I would have chipped a needle
from my bone, undone every sinew
in me to stitch up the wound in you.
And it was only later, home, you
woozing on the sofa, that I knew
how close you'd come to being gone.
I understand today

that we're in different terminals
heading opposite directions,
and I can not pinch this distance closed
with tender thumbs. There's no staunch or stitch
or suture I can cry out for
for this. This is how our hurts come down.
Hard and without warning.

Outbreak

By chance, when all the country's news is floods,
this city's struck by weeping in the streets,
and who knows where the grief first overtopped?
The woman with the phone hard at her chest
as if to prove her heart was still in it
to someone listening in the bus she held
against her shoulder-blades, half-way pulled-out
across the carriageway, for near an hour
until a hi-vis gang could tear her off
and let the bus, its passengers, depart?
The man outside the church? The woman prone
beside the cash machine? I swear, when some-
one first says 'epidemic' on the news
we're done for, neighbour. We will not be stopped.

Portrait of Poet with Dimmer Switch

Of all the home improvements he could make
he has made one – the installation of
a dimmer switch set in his writing desk
which, calibrated automatically,
maintains the light indoors a notch below
the light outside. This way he does not have
to see himself reflected in the glass
or, round him, all the things that prove him home.

This way he can address the changing of
the seasons and not once come up against
the two-faced, God-damned falsehood he's become.
The daylight hours and summer months are fine
but afternoons' and autumns' drawings-in
precurse the wastes of hours spent in the dark.

He will describe the moon and stars, the sun,
the streetlights, from his window seat, and fail
to see the one illuminating thing;
whatever light out here falls in on him.

'Go call your sorrows to the lapwing'

Go call your sorrows to the lapwing.

Go call your sorrows to the curlew.

Go call your sorrows to the godwit.

Go call your sorrows to the plover.

Go call your sorrows to the bittern.

Go call your sorrows to the woodcock.

Go call your sorrows to the corncrake.

Dymock

for Matthew

i.

I shouldn't like to say that what you saw
was not a Golden Oriole for sure

but see, the field guide does seem to suggest
that we are many counties too far west

and if, to name that dash of green, I swore
I knew that it was gold- or fire-crest

I'd more than likely have mistaken it.

The day is too far gone to learn much more.
It's but a little way back to our door

once I have nursed my breath against a wall.
The bull is madding in his metal stall.

I'm troubled by a cough. Let's go, before
a dusking bird I can not name at all

starts making plain I have forsaken it.

ii.

For all the blossom puffing up the trees,
for all the happy uproar of the bees

I'd trade this day in May for one in June
but should I have my wish, no doubt, too soon

I'd hanker for an endless August day
and in a breath wish that whole month away

for windfall-wasps and fires of fallen leaves
and then I'd conjure frost onto the eaves

and snow, and with it all December's hush
then wist for thaw and first green things to rush

to bud and bloom and occupy the bees
uproariously blossoming in trees.

And this is how we hasten ourselves on.
How eagerly we wish our few days gone.

iii.

This final sun-stretched afternoon we walk,
we two, between the houses of the dead
then hill-down, field-edge, brook-bank, furrow tread
and listen for the cadence of their talk
in all we find we have to talk about.
We have not been this way before, but should.
And all the guns that busy in the wood
and fighters overhead can't drown it out.

But soon will come a stile or gate that you
or I must climb to take a different path
and all along your homeward grass or earth
by field by farther field, keep talking through
the clamour of the trees and all the birds,
please; even if I can't make out the words.

iv.

And up beyond the nettle-wrack, away
from broad-leaved ruin of the keeper's cote
through bluebell, beech and all the under-rot
of garlic wilding in the yellowed day

and up into the copse of pines on top
of May Hill through the wind that wallops you
and chops your hands to vegetable blue
and lofts the rook and hawk in gyre and drop

and up above the Severn vale and twelve
bright counties in their greens and yellow greens;
and this is more of earth than we have seen
at once, at all, of sky or of ourselves

and so we mark up bench or skin or book
with blade or blood or ink, for good; come look.

Torch Song

                                she is
so pleased to discover that
those astronauts had planted
cats' eyes across the near side
of the moon –
                if you catch her
on her back on the night-lawn
with a strong torch she will be
testing quite how far from things
she is

Neighbours

for Julia

They never lock their homes this far from town.
He lives alone next-door to her alone.
They only see each other out-of-doors,
incurious acquaintances for years.

A chance remark from her, across the bins,
in tears, and he pops round, lets himself in
while she is out, with half a glass of wine
to leave beside her tissues and her phone.

He moans about the night-long owls and she
comes over with a sketch of him asleep –
stick-man amid a crowd of zeds and stars –
and weights it with two earplugs on his stairs.

She mentions that she's heard a song she likes
and, two days later, early, she awakes
to find a new disc spinning out the tune
through grand new speakers in her living room.

And this is how a thing can escalate –
from her to him, in time of rain, a boat;
while no acknowledgement, no thanks is said;
from him to her, her likeness cast in gold;

and no, this will not end with them in bed;
from her to him, from him to her, the world.

Host

There comes a knock at the door
or, in fact, one low wet slap
and queued across the garden
are frogs, maybe all the frogs.

Look at all your wide wet eyes!

Come in, she hears herself croak,
and they do come in, sad-faced
and travel-sore and she helps
the weakest over the mat.

Mi casa, su casa, friends!

She sets the bath taps running,
lets water swamp the carpet
and throws the windows open
for the flies, the doors for slugs.

You frogs with your funny ways!

She's gardening more these days,
lies some nights beneath the trees,
hours watching her unlit house,
unsure how this came about.

Revelator

The time has come and we are not prepared.
We are the dead-to-life that none can raise.
We are the beasts turned from the ark, unpaired.
We howl that this is not the end of days.

National Park

This gate you're leaning on is more or less
the place we'll put the Welcome area.
That barn converts into the platform for
a monorail – in sympathetic green
and brown – down to the Heart of the Forest,
with an audio-loop to name the trees
and point out spotlit burrows, setts and dreys,
the nesting-sites of the rarer birds, with
a subtle soundtrack of Elgar and bees.
Can we do something about this rain? So,
parking. A gift shop. Toilets. Some monkeys.

Angry Mob Confronts Poet

Here, slot the last coin in the telescope.
We've chosen you to take the longer view,
so do. We'll hold your sweater and your coat.

North, at Scarborough cliffs, is there perhaps
a woman clinging to a neon board
that spells out *The Grand Hot-* amid the flood?

And further still, maybe a polar bear
obsessing at its circus trick atop
the water, balanced on its stunt of ice?

And does the magnifying of your point
of view exacerbate the tilting-down
we think we've sensed along the island's length?

A penny only goes so far. The clock-
work shutter-mechanism ticks and ticks
until the sudden snap of its eclipse.

We're right behind you still, though, till it drops.
You will be sure to turn and tell us all
about it, won't you, when your time is up?

Token

When the boys came back with a disk of ice
prised from the mouth of a water-butt,
they'd taken turns with its slippery weight
across the hills and down towards the house:

a riot shield, a lighthouse lens, a wheel
from the Snow Queen's chariot, the shed skin
of the moon, a puddle closed for business,
the plug of a polar fishing-hole,

a sequin from a glacier's wedding train,
a rune, a superhero's hover-board,
a cymbal, a baffle, an almost-naught,
a store-house of one summer morning's rain,

a keyless portal to the underworld,
a coin to toss to choose between weathers,
a cataract, a long-playing record
of all the sound that water ever made.

In truth, we were afraid we could not think
what we should make of it, and turned away
and busied ourselves so as not to see
the hours and hours it took to come to nothing.

Same Old

This will be a poem about a man
who'll wake to a morning bright with ground-mist
and walk himself into the orange light
over field after field brittle with frost

and think himself lost very close to home,
stop by what seems the dead end of a stream
to watch the water turn beneath the ice,
half-hearing from far off a single crow,

and who, turning from his thoughts, will startle
from the gorse-lee a pair of snipe to lift
in a glittering rush, to panic off,
low across the meadow, and disappear

and he will receive his epiphany
here of how unbearable beauty is
and here we'll leave him and no one will say
how he will have to go about his day.

Star Slime

This end is one I'll know:
snapped in the beak of Crow,

Frog, burst aloft by Death,
who in her closing breath

confesses all in blurts.
Her all-at-once of hurts

is a transparent spoor
of slime across the moor.

Clap-trapper, Hollow-bones,
drop my skin among stones.

All I will leave's remorse
hung, fruitless, in the gorse.

Close

ii

Everything is coming clear;
that blackbird set deep in
the shrinking tree, a cell,
a shadow hymning in
the accumulating dusk.

I Lay This at Your Feet

Here, I have pounced upon
the darting creature – Love.

It hid and feinted, fled,
rolled over and played dead.

But see, I've pinned it down –
how neatly pinned it down –

carried it in tender teeth.
I lay this at your feet.

About Today

Dust storms swept in from the Sahara, March 2014

The carriage was too hot
and everyone was fractious
by the time we came to halt
somewhere near Birmingham.

I was already in floods
before the storm of red dust
blew its way into the train
and made the matter worse.

Of course, we were moved on
in time, the dust did settle.
I think I smell of desert
but I'm here, brushed off. All right.

I've tried to save some for you
in the corner of my eye –
in a trembling drop a speck
you'll have to get in close to see.

Harlequin

In the days since the coming of the snow
you've been around the house performing mimes:
in a doorway, the scooping-up of water
with both hands in a time of drought;
in the kitchen, the supplicant's stretch
to the back of a truck for a bag of rice;
on your knees under the table, at prayer,
your hair loose and pouring into your palms;

and all the while what you've been getting at
is a ladybird, which you've saved and saved
and lifted to various disused shelves
and will not put out in the snow.
I play my part in this act of kindness,
turning down the radio and its news
that one species is killing off the rest,
though you no more than I know which this is.

Anniversary in Fort Augustus

Love, we came for a monster, didn't we? –
drove nine hours through worsening light and weather
and found ourselves beside the beaten loch

squinting at branch, or goose, or trick of mist
far out in the snowfall on the water
and watched each other whiting out in fog

and knew the hunt, for now, was at a loss.
Icy stones along the shore made walking
hard, and we propped each other when a stag,

far off and out of sight, began to sound
the valley's depth and the depth of winter,
the lowing echoes following us back

to a door with a latch, a hearth with fire
to keep us through nights and years of wolving.

Leaving

v. The Hill of the Muses

This is how I take you with me;
by saying to the empty seat
beside me – Look! how orange is
the sun above the sea; now squint
to squeeze its circle from the glare,

and look! over your shoulder, how
the Parthenon squares up to it
and whelms itself with orange light –
before the sun, the heat and you
and I all go down together.

I take it you are lost for words
through pines and aloe vera to
the streetlights and the orange trees
as I watch your steps and wonder –
What d'you think? What d'you make of that?

Leaving

There's not one drop of happiness more
to be sucked out of the afternoon
than to see you fish a quartered lime
out of your drink and wince at the taste
and shunt an ice-cube out of the way
with the two long, white straws you're using
to squeeze the life from a glass of mint.

London to Leeds

I can see that I am beside myself.
Suffer me to sleep on the luggage shelf.

My temple buffers at the window-glass
as house- and street-lights constellate and pass –

south or north of Grantham, late at night –
by this carriage quite deserted and bright.

You'll know this by now

how we wait, and how
we listen
for a homing noise
at the door –
letterbox-tattle,
lock-rattle;
and the way our love
for our loves
makes us fear as much
for the ones
on the morning bus
as for those
in helicopters,
landing-craft;
or how an invite
on the mat
bangs down loud as the
telegram
when they're out, at war
or the shop;
you'll know this because
you've opened
a door, once, and heard
or said, *Hi,*
love, I'm home, and known
for sure that
that is why we'll wait
for the knocks
or a ring and know
that we'll take
anything

Found

You are held
in a queue

Someone will
be with you

Advent

O little child, o child to come
knocking at the world's door, for whom,
still, your small universe of womb
is all there is to know, strike dumb
the voices of our worldly gloom;
no room, no room, no room.

O little child, make good the sum
of human love. Of every crumb
create a thousand shares. Presume
this much, at least, that there's one home
from which the answer will not come,
no room, no room, no room.

Suburban

The day that him-over-the-back
leaned over his good fence and said
that someone in the night had dragged
a garden chair against the boards,
to vault through our tree's disorder
and trespass across our borders –

the day we paid a bloke to hack
the hawthorn hedge we later heard,
from her-across-the-way, had wrecked
her views, for years, across our yard
and down to where our suburb cedes
to the next grey ward into Leeds –

was the day we solved the tracks:
we drove home late and by the drive
our cats faced down a brace of fox
in the arena of our lights
in the run between the common
and our street of ransacked wheelie-bins.

They were not fighting and they were
not hackled up, and we unlocked
and locked ourselves indoors and saw
them deadlocked from each room we blacked.
And now we can not tell how deep,
how fast, how still we are to sleep.

Waves

Turn off the radio, please – I can't take
one more story of a parent and kids
ripped from a shore or upturned in a loch,
of how not all, or none, came swimming back –

not now I've put our boy once in the sea
balanced on my forearm to kick kick kick
and watched him grow accustomed to the shocks
of buoyancy in waves hard at his back.

Please – my head is full of helicopters.
I know, I know. He will let go of me.

Suburban

iii. Keeping Bees

Another thing we would not do:
keep a box of busy-bodies
to tangle with our overgrowth
or gang up on the neighbours' stocks;
not with our cats and two-year-old,
the fox who knows to lift the lid,
not with such indifferent weather,
the pesticides, the mites, the risk
of anaphylaxis, the estate's
opprobrium, its blank windows,
not with the brothers hanging out
of their back bedroom, gun glinting.

Mercy

I cut its head off with a kitchen knife
while you were out.

It didn't fight. Its spine went with a crack.
There was more blood

than I'd have thought. Before you ask, I don't
know how I could.

It's just, this is what we do. It was quick.
It was past help.

Fifteen years is a long time, isn't it?
I bagged it up

and took it to the outside bin – I was
very sad, yes –

and washed and dried its bowl, the chopping board
by hand and went

into the living room to face our son,
explain myself.

It has rained all week

and you've set down the things you have to say
of love and home and of your baby boy
and shut your book and put your pen away
and, outside, nothing is but green and grey,
so wet with rain that it must never dry.

It's later than you thought, and what remains
but this? to walk out past the raspberry canes
barefoot, to drop your sweater on the lawn,
to cast off everything along the lane,
wade into open country and the rain.

And at the tree-line turn but once to look
at where you've come from, if you will, then back
into the nearer birch and farther oak
and know your skin is stiffening with bark
or bristling with fur. The wood is dark

and all you know of love and all of pain
is falling from you. All you know is rain.

When the time comes

                let's unscrew the front door
from its hinges, careless of our landlord,
and leave the wind and snow to nose around
and settle down into our empty home.
Let's drag it off to the edge of the hill
at the last gasp of dusk and set it down
and sit upon the uphill panel. Now,
fit your heels, darling, in the letterbox
and take the handle lightly in your hand
and I'll squeeze in behind you, belt my arms
around your chest, and we'll let ourselves go.

And snow will foam on either side, and frogs
and mice and all the common creatures leap
out of our path. Whatever words are left
to us are sucked out of our lungs and torn
to nothing by the westering storm and we
accelerate into our only way.

It's just a thought. A door into the dark.
I can not think how I could love you more.

Last Word

I'm fucking off now to leave you in peace,
to take my excuses out through the trees,
into the river and, there, on my knees
I'll explain everything to the geese.